Judy Blume
It's not the end of the world

I0817463

A DELL YEARLING BOOK
Tales of a Fourth Grade Nothing
Judy Blume

A DELL YEARLING BOOK
Otherwise Known as Sheila the Great
Judy Blume

DELL 1.50
DEENIE
JUDY BLUME

A DELL YEARLING BOOK $1.50
Blubber
Judy Blume

DELL 1.50
Starring Sally J. Freedman As Herself
Judy Blume

might be

To Judy Blume, forever.

Christy Ottaviano and Marietta Zacker, you are both so wonderful for believing in this project from the get-go. I also must thank friends who helped along the way: Aya Gordon Noy, Leslie Margolis, Adrienne Vrettos, Lisa Desimini, Sarah Lynne Reul, and Abby Hanlon. And to my mom, for letting me read whatever I wanted.

About This Book

The illustrations for this book were done in acrylic and collage on Bristol board. This book was edited by Christy Ottaviano and designed by Brenda E. Angelilli. The production was supervised by Kimberly Stella, and the production editors were Marisa Finkelstein and JoAnna Kremer. The text was set in Sassoon Infant Regular, and the display type is Bernhard Gothic URW Ultra.

 Christy Ottaviano Books • Hachette Book Group • 1290 Avenue of the Americas, New York, NY 10104 • Visit us at LBYR .com • First Edition: February 2026 • Christy Ottaviano Books is an imprint of Little, Brown and Company. • The Christy Ottaviano Books name and logo are registered trademarks of Hachette Book Group, Inc. • The publisher is not responsible for websites (or their content) that are not owned by the publisher. • Little, Brown and Company books may be purchased in bulk for business, educational, or promotional use. For information, please contact your local bookseller or the Hachette Book Group Special Markets Department at special.markets@hbgusa.com. • Library of Congress Cataloging-in-Publication Data • Names: Alko, Selina, author, illustrator. • Title: Otherwise known as Judy the Great : a poetic ode to Judy Blume / by Selina Alko. • Description: First edition. | New York : Little, Brown and Company, 2026. | "Christy Ottaviano Books." | Includes bibliographical references. | Audience term: Children | Audience: Ages 6–10. | Summary: A collection of poems that honor the childhood years of Judy Blume. • Identifiers: LCCN 2024060434 | ISBN 9780316570633 (hardcover) • Subjects: LCSH: Children's poetry, American. | CYAC: Blume, Judy—Poetry. | American poetry. | LCGFT: Biographical poetry. | Picture books. • Classification: LCC PS3601.L3975 O84 2025 | DDC 811/.54—dc23/eng/20250207 • LC record available at https://lccn.loc .gov/2024060434 • ISBN 978-0-316-57063-3 • PRINTED IN DONGGUAN, CHINA • APS, 10/25 • 10 9 8 7 6 5 4 3 2 1

Otherwise Known as JUDY THE GREAT

A Poetic Ode to JUDY BLUME

Selina Alko

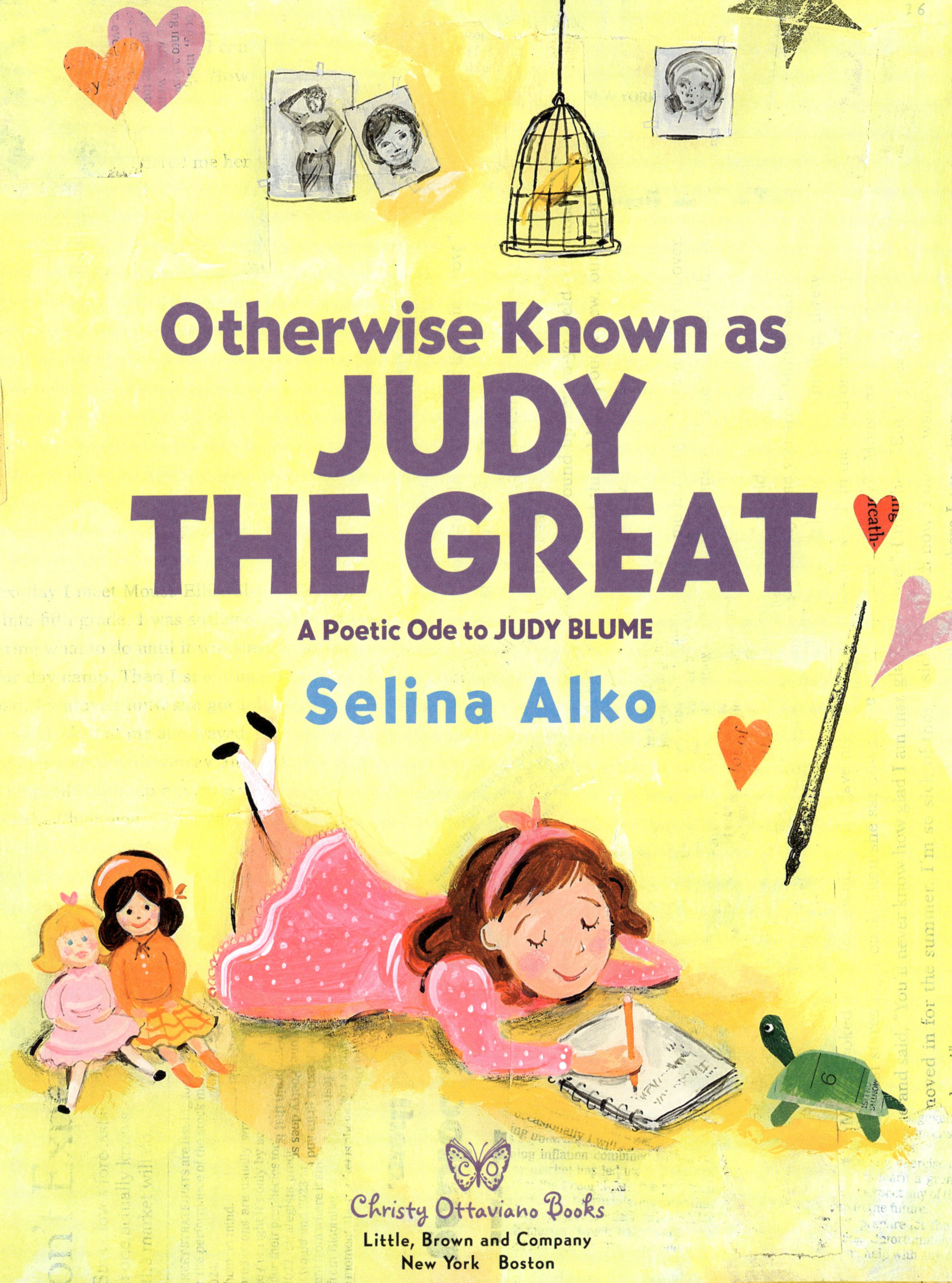

Christy Ottaviano Books
Little, Brown and Company
New York Boston

Judy the Great

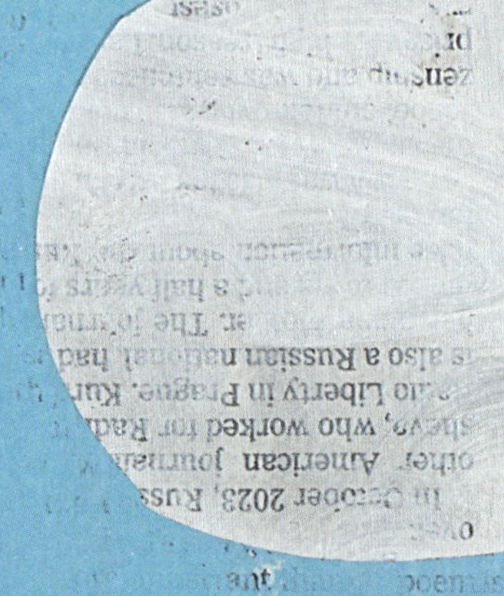

Two days away
from Valentine's Day
in an otherwise quiet town,
a girl who would grow up
to be a great writer is born.
The date is February 12, 1938.
The town is Elizabeth, New Jersey.
The girl is Judith Sussman.
Otherwise known as Judy the Great.

ESSIE
RUDY
NANNY MAMA
DAVID
JUDY

Close-Knit

Like strands of wool in a sweater,
        Judy's family was close-knit.
Her father at the head,
        Rudolph or "Rudy,"
connecting the sleeves.
Judy's mom,
Esther or "Essie,"
and her grandmother, "Nanny Mama,"
all hold tight to the children—
David and Judy
siblings, opposites,
in the belly of the cardigan.

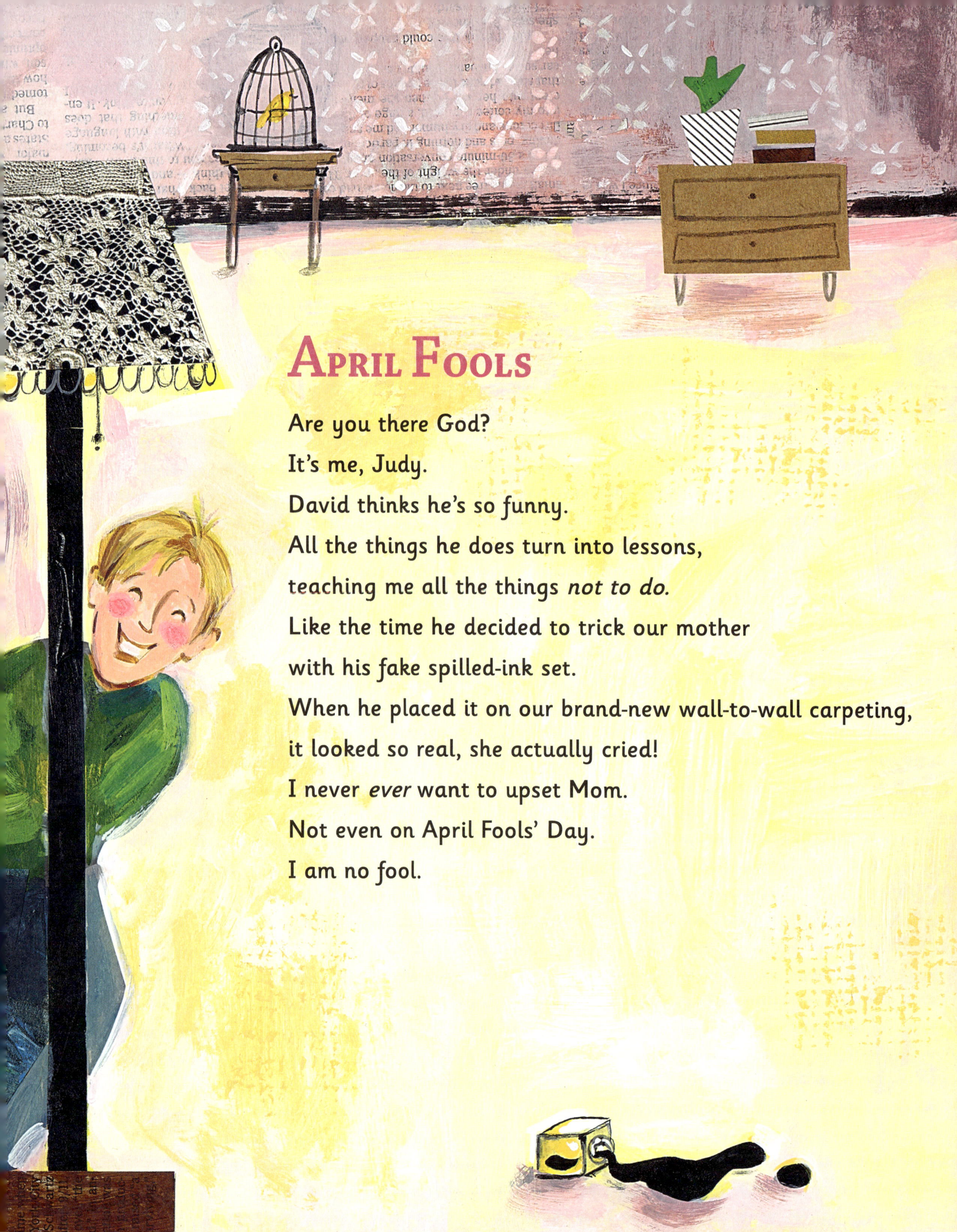

April Fools

Are you there God?
It's me, Judy.
David thinks he's so funny.
All the things he does turn into lessons,
teaching me all the things *not to do.*
Like the time he decided to trick our mother
with his fake spilled-ink set.
When he placed it on our brand-new wall-to-wall carpeting,
it looked so real, she actually cried!
I never *ever* want to upset Mom.
Not even on April Fools' Day.
I am no fool.

Perfect

Judy kept quiet.

She *rarely* got in trouble.

Little. Miss. Perfect.

Rudy

Really
Upstanding
Dentist.
Youngest of
        not one,
        not two,
        not three,
but SEVEN siblings.
Everyone—including Judy—
brought their problems to Rudy.
Judy adored Rudy,
and Rudy adored Judy.
        Was she her daddy's girl?
        Naturally.

Family Dinner

On Friday nights at six,
Essie might fix:
chopped liver with schmaltz
on crackers or rye . . .
Those were the appetizers
you *had* to try . . .
Dinner was next,
a feast for the eyes . . .
pot roast,
roast chicken,
potatoes or fries . . .

Then—
a treat,
something sweet,
a delicious chocolate layer cake.
(Everyone knew Essie could bake!)

Freckle Juice

Are you there God?
    It's me, Judy.
I want to be a glamorous movie star.
Margaret O'Brien and Esther Williams are my idols, by far.
There is also Doris Day,
whose freckles portray
    a vision of beauty and film noir.

What if I mix ketchup, mustard, and onion until it settles,
then add olive oil, salt and pepper in speckles,
blend in vinegar and grape juice,
mayonnaise and lemon juice . . .
    Will I, too,
    get freckles?

Mama's Helper

Judy set five china teacups
and saucers on a silver platter.

Four of Essie's friends were coming over.
Judy steadily poured
One. Cup. At. A. Time
and then carried each teacup
One. Step. At. A. Time
to each one of the ladies.

Uh-oh!
The last teacup
tipped
over
and fell.
Essie—to her credit—did not yell.
But she was upset. Judy just knew.
What was a mama's helper to do?
Sop up the liquid
One. Wipe. At. A. Time.

Holidays

To Judy, Christmas was pure magic.
The flashy lights, the decorations—the whole schtick.
It wasn't Judy's holiday, but she didn't mind,
since Hanukkah brought gifts of its own kind.
The best day ever was when Essie took Judy
to go shopping in New York City.
Twenty-seven minutes by train to Penn Station,
a day in "the City" was like a vacation.
Gifts were picked out by Essie and Judy
for Nanny Mama, Judy's friends, David, and Rudy.
Then after lunch, the two of them would go
to the latest, most exciting Broadway show!
Later, Essie and Judy had one last thing to see:
the Rockefeller Center Christmas Tree.

Finian's Rainbow
Paperback Row

Tales of a Fourth Grade Reader

The very best gift Essie gave to Judy
was letting her read whatever she wanted.

And Judy wanted to read
whatever she could get her hands on,
be it cereal boxes
or serial stories—

Judy read as much as she could.

She loved escaping to the public library
to feed her imagination.

By fourth grade she bought a book a week
with her allowance money.

Wizards and scarecrows,
tinmen and lions
turned to movies in Judy's mind.

Betsy-Tacy friendship adventures
and Nancy Drew mysteries

kept Judy close company
like a band of best friends.

MADELINE
THE MYSTERY OF THE 99 STEPS
NANCY DREW
43
GROSSET & DUNLAP
THE SECRET OF THE OLD CLOCK
NANCY DREW
1
GROSSET & DUNLAP
BETSY-TACY
The MAGIC of OZ
BAUM
Reilly & Lee
The Wizard of Oz
Baum
Reilly & Lee

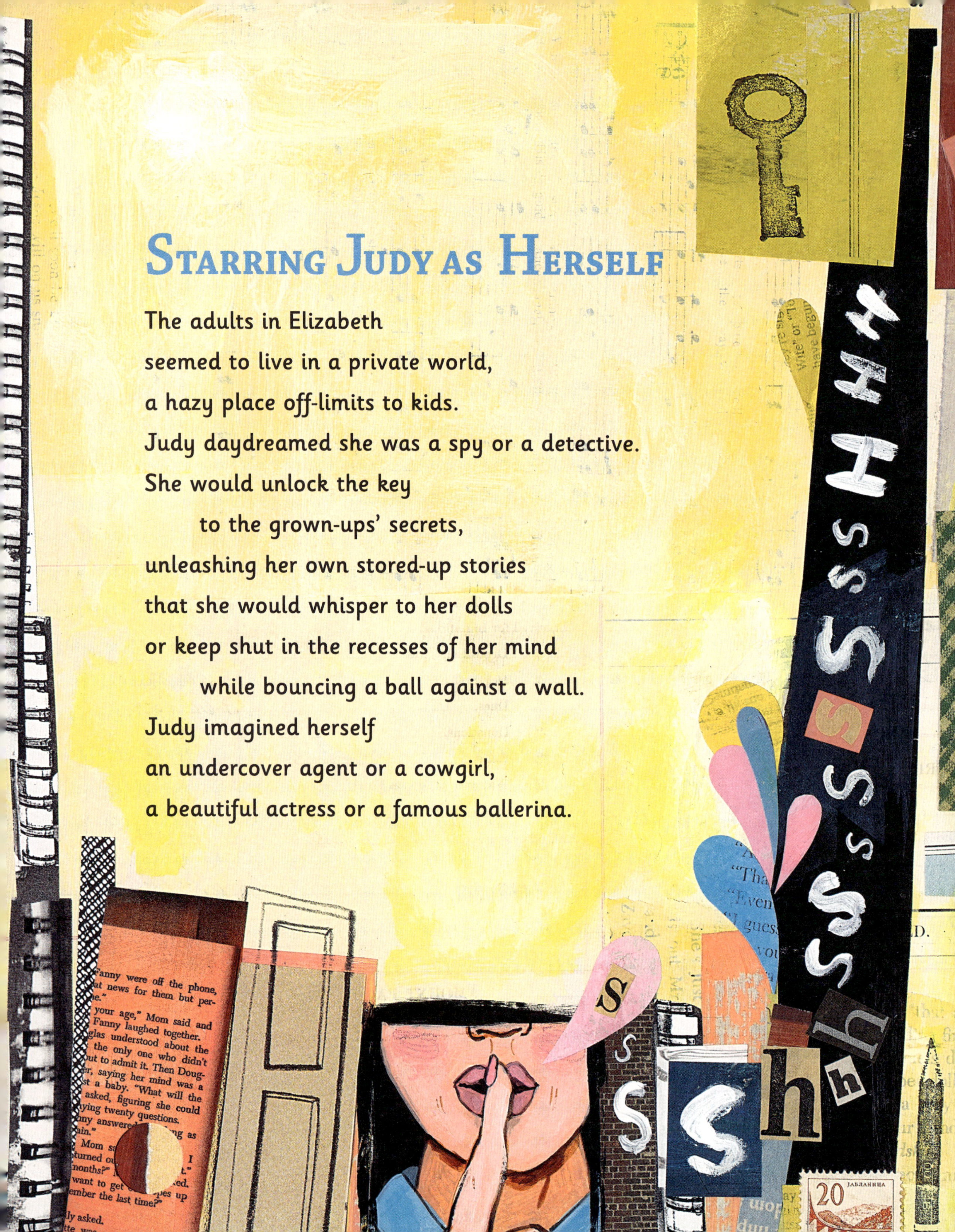

Starring Judy as Herself

The adults in Elizabeth
seemed to live in a private world,
a hazy place off-limits to kids.
Judy daydreamed she was a spy or a detective.
She would unlock the key
        to the grown-ups' secrets,
unleashing her own stored-up stories
that she would whisper to her dolls
or keep shut in the recesses of her mind
        while bouncing a ball against a wall.
Judy imagined herself
an undercover agent or a cowgirl,
a beautiful actress or a famous ballerina.

She was always brave,
always strong.
In her imagination,
Judy was always the hero.

Always the **STAR.**

World War II

Are you there God?

It's me, Judy.

World War II is *always* on the radio.
Even though it's happening overseas,
over there, far away . . .
it feels close to home.
News of food rationing, sirens, bombings,
and BAD THINGS happening to the Jews—

our ancestors,

Jewish people,

just like our family,

floats through our living room
like a bad smell.
God, if you end the War soon,
I don't need to be a movie star.

Thanks for listening.

NEW
DAY
known
year
THE NEW YORK TIMES

It's Not the End of the World

When Judy was nine,
David fell sick.

As a guide,
the doctor prescribed:

palm trees, sandy beaches,
hibiscus flowers, and peaches,

warm breezes, leisure time,
fresh air, and sunshine.

Nanny Mama and the family
—except for Rudy,
who had to work—

packed their bags
and took the train far away.
Not to the end of the world,
but far enough away from the cold,
to Miami Beach, Florida.

The Sunshine State was good for David's health,
and it was good for Judy, too.

She discovered swimming, bike riding, roller-skating sessions,
cartwheels, weird bugs, and ballet lessons.

If only Judy didn't still worry about her father,
all alone
back at home.

Then Again, Maybe He Will Be Next

Once David recovered,
the Sussmans moved back to Elizabeth
where it seemed to Judy,
one of Rudy's siblings was always dying.
Shiva in Hebrew means "seven."
For seven straight days
after someone Jewish dies
family and friends
gather where the loved one lived
to *sit shiva*,
sitting and eating and mourning
the departed.
While everyone else
sat and ate and mourned,
Judy sat and ate and worried.
Would her daddy be next?

6
5
4
3
2
1
COURSE OF EXCHANGE.
LONDON, 19th OCTOBER, 1911.
EXCHANGE.
3.24.19
48
Rome
It all goes back to Christmas Day
hink back to the last time you
HALVAH
"Don't worry."

Unlikely Events

In quiet Elizabeth, unlikely events rarely happened. Until one winter—not one but TWO airplanes crashed to the ground. ***Had aliens invaded?*** Judy worried. Her fears swirled in her head like a ring around Saturn. She didn't dare voice her concerns out loud. She didn't dare disturb the adults who were already disturbed by the unlikely events. Judy willed her worries far away. Way out into outer space. Judy tried as hard as she could to will herself to act ordinary.

But then, the following month,
a THIRD flying metal vessel fell from the sky!
Judy was terrified. ***Had Martians landed in her hometown?***
Loud noises and big bangs made Judy jumpy. Soon, Rudy was
summoned for his dental expertise, to identify the victims' remains.
Judy never forgot the fear of that year, but she did
her very best to smile and carry on.

Bargains

Are you there God?
It's me, Judy.
If I follow all the rules,
will you protect our town from aliens?

God, can you hear me?
It's Judy.
If I brush my teeth twice a day,
will you keep my family safe?

Are you there God?
It's me, Judy, again.
If I get a hundred on my math test,
will you especially watch over my daddy?

FAKE BOOK REPORT
A
To Judy, many books written for kids were boring.
She was sick of the same old stories
about girls and horses
or girls on farms with more horses.
Where were the stories about girls like her?
A city girl.
Or the stories about girls with her same problems?
City problems.
Where were the real stories about real people?
The books about things that really happened?
One day at school,
Judy invented a book to write about.
Maybe it was a fake book report,
but it felt real to Judy.
And—much to her surprise—
on the report, she got an A!
What does that say?
Maybe Judy was on to something . . .

Ode to Her Pen

Judy loved her pen the most.
She always kept it close.
Judy's pen
was her faithful friend.

Pre-Teen Kittens

Judy's friends were changing,
and she was changing, too.
Judy had so many questions.
She couldn't find answers
from any of the adults.
So Judy and her best friends formed a club.
They would get to the bottom of things!
Comparing notes over Cokes
and rows of Oreos,
the "Pre-Teen Kittens"
shared *all* their woes.

END OF SENTENCE

Are you there God?
    It's me, Judy.
I can't wait to be more grown-up.
I am so excited!
I can hardly hide it.
If not this afternoon,
God, please let *it* happen soon.

PERIOD.
End of sentence.

leaving
stories
PAST

Novels
sincere
love
welcome
wonder
NYU
novelist
imaginative life
FUTURE.

BOOK REVIEW 13
Fudge-a-Mania
Double Fudge
Cool Zone
Going Going Gone
Friend or Fiend
Here's to You Rachel Robinson
Freckle Juice
Blubber
Tiger Eyes
Deenie
Forever
In the Unlikely Event
Judy Blume

Judy Blooms

As Judy grew up,
new branches of her life brought
college and marriage and motherhood.
Now known as Judy Blume,
she observed her young children,
a boy and a girl,
and she remembered her own childhood.
New ideas came to her,
flooding through her past,
shedding light over her shut-in feelings.
Judy wanted to dig up the truth
of being a young person.
She wished to write stories for kids,
to help them navigate their lives,
to help them grow up.
Judy yearned to be a professional writer—
an *Author*.
One day,
Judy sat down at her desk,
pressing letters into words,
then words into sentences.
And not right away,
but soon,
Judy's stories
one by one
would break out and

BLOOM.

Author's Note

Judy Blume's books were *everything* to me growing up in Vancouver, Canada, in the 1970s. Her stories taught me about life, love, heartbreak, families, and friendship. I would read them over and over, often late into the night, identifying with her characters, whose interior monologues, thoughts, feelings, and obsessions often mirrored my own. In a way, Judy Blume helped raise me.

Over fifty years ago, her stories exploded onto the scene, resonating with millions of kids around the world, and her books remain beloved today. How did she do it? I think the best way to understand her success is by looking at the seeds planted in her childhood. Who was Judy Blume growing up?

In exploring Judy's life, I came across a few signficant experiences that seemed to spark her growing worries. As a secular Jew living in an American suburb, Judy listened to President Roosevelt's World War II reports on the radio as evening entertainment with her family, and they often sat shiva for their relatives. I was also astounded to learn that in Judy's hometown of Elizabeth, New Jersey, there had been three airplane crashes in one year. Apparently, these tragedies were not talked about or explained to Judy at the time. She was expected to cope with these difficult events by pretending they didn't happen. It became clear to me why Judy turned inward—honing her imagination, becoming a writer even in childhood. It is no wonder she wrote such realistic, truth-telling characters in her novels for kids later on.

Although I grew up in Canada thirty years after Judy, similarly I was a Jewish child with a big imagination. Like Judy, I read Nancy Drew and the Wizard of Oz books,

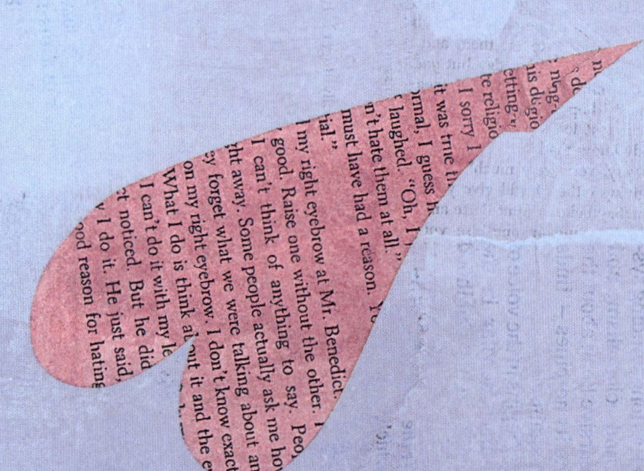

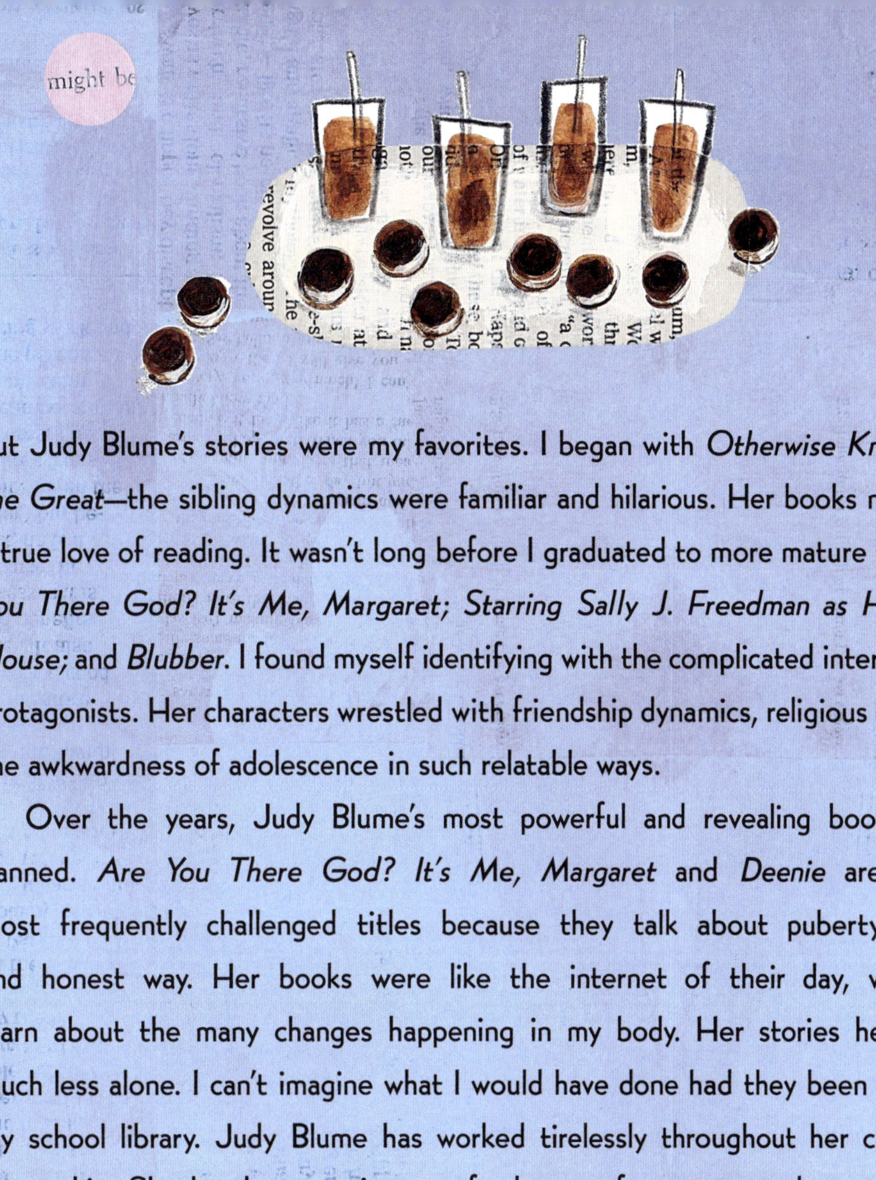

but Judy Blume's stories were my favorites. I began with *Otherwise Known as Sheila the Great*—the sibling dynamics were familiar and hilarious. Her books nurtured in me a true love of reading. It wasn't long before I graduated to more mature titles, like *Are You There God? It's Me, Margaret; Starring Sally J. Freedman as Herself; Iggie's House;* and *Blubber*. I found myself identifying with the complicated interior lives of her protagonists. Her characters wrestled with friendship dynamics, religious questions, and the awkwardness of adolescence in such relatable ways.

Over the years, Judy Blume's most powerful and revealing books have been banned. *Are You There God? It's Me, Margaret* and *Deenie* are two of her most frequently challenged titles because they talk about puberty in an open and honest way. Her books were like the internet of their day, where I could learn about the many changes happening in my body. Her stories helped me feel much less alone. I can't imagine what I would have done had they been removed from my school library. Judy Blume has worked tirelessly throughout her career to fight censorship. She has been a pioneer of advocacy for young readers at the onset of a growing movement to suppress expression in young people's literature, which sadly continues today.

I hope that this book will motivate a new generation of young readers and writers to get to know the trailblazing author Judy Blume. Maybe they will see themselves in young Judy's childhood. Or maybe they will be inspired in other ways by the one and only Judy Blume, otherwise known as Judy the Great!

Selina

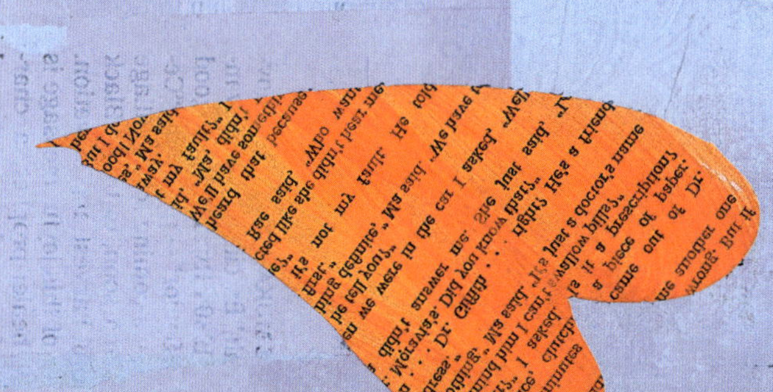

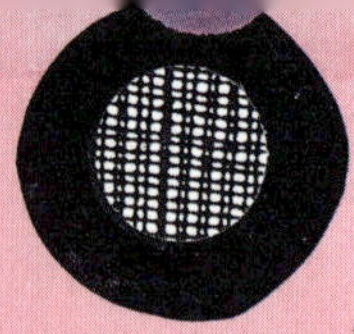

TIMELINE

February 12, 1938: Judy is born Judith Sussman in Elizabeth, New Jersey.

1939: World War II begins in Europe.

1947: Judy's family moves to Miami Beach, Florida (for two years).

1951–52: Three airplanes crash in Elizabeth, New Jersey (within three months).

1959: Judy marries John Blume. Judy's father dies.

1961: Judy graduates from New York University. Judy's daughter, Randy, is born.

1963: Judy's son, Lawrence, is born.

1969: Judy publishes her first book, *The One in the Middle Is the Green Kangaroo.*

1970: *Iggie's House* and *Are You There God? It's Me, Margaret* are published.

1971: *Then Again, Maybe I Won't* and *Freckle Juice* are published.

1972: *It's Not the End of the World, Tales of a Fourth Grade Nothing,* and *Otherwise Known as Sheila the Great* are published.

1973: *Deenie* is published.

1974: *Blubber* is published. "The Pain and the Great One" is published as a poem in *Free to Be You and Me.*

1975: Judy and John Blume divorce. *Forever...* is published as a young adult novel.

1976: Judy marries Thomas Kitchens (ends in divorce in 1978).

1977: *Starring Sally J. Freedman as Herself*, Judy's most autobiographical book, is published.

1978: *Wifey** is published.

1980: *Superfudge* is published.

1981: *Tiger Eyes* is published.

1983: *Smart Women** is published.

1984: *The Pain and the Great One* is published as a novel.

1986: *Letters to Judy: What Kids Wish They Could Tell You** is published.

1987: Judy marries George Cooper. *Just as Long as We're Together* is published.

1990: *Fudge-a-mania* is published.

1993: *Here's to You, Rachel Robinson* is published.

1998: *Summer Sisters** is published.

2000: Judy Blume is named a Living Legend by the Library of Congress.

2002: *Double Fudge* is published.

2007: *Soupy Saturdays with the Pain and the Great One* is published.

2008: *Cool Zone with the Pain and the Great One* and *Going, Going, Gone! with the Pain and the Great One* are published.

2009: *Friend or Fiend? with the Pain and the Great One* is published.

2015: *In The Unlikely Event** is published.

2016: Judy and George open Books & Books bookstore in Key West, Florida.

*Books written for an adult readership.

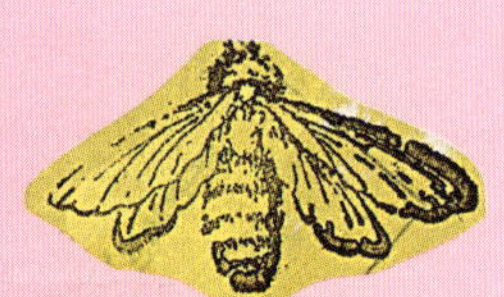

SOURCES

Anderson, Kirsten. *Who Is Judy Blume?* New York, NY: Penguin Workshop, 2018.

Bergstein, Rachel. *The Genius of Judy: How Judy Blume Rewrote Childhood for All of Us.* New York, NY. Simon & Schuster, 2024.

Blume, Judy. *Letters to Judy: What Your Kids Wish They Could Tell You.* New York, NY: G. P. Putnam's Sons, 1986.

Krull, Kathleen. *Judy Blume: Are You There, Reader? It's Me, Judy!* Women Who Broke the Rules series: New York, NY: Bloomsbury, 2015.

Mead, Wendy. *Judy Blume: Spotlight on Children's Authors.* New York, NY: Cavendish Square, 2015.

Pardo, Davina, and Leah Wolchok, dir. *Judy Blume Forever.* Amazon Prime, 2023.

Sperling, Nicole. "How Judy Blume Finally Got a 'Yes' from Hollywood." *The New York Times,* March 7, 2023.

Judy with her father, mother, and grandmother

Judy and her brother, David, on their way to see the Goodyear Blimp

Judy outside her store, Books & Books, in Key West, Florida

Judy Blume
TIGER EYES
A DELL YEARLING BOOK 3.25
Judy Blume
Superfudge
DELL YEARLING
$3.25
Judy Blume
THE PAIN and THE GREATONE
JUDY BLUME
FUDGE-a-MANIA
Five
Just as Long as We're Together
JUDY BLUME
JUDY BLUME
HERE'S TO YOU, RACHEL ROBINSON